CREATE A SUCCESSFUL BUSINESS WEBSITE

FRANKIE J. FOSTER

PUBLISHED BY FRANKIE J. FOSTER

CREATE A SUCCESSFUL BUSINESS WEBSITE

Step-by-Step Approach

First Impressions Matter

Your website's design is a major factor in deciding the credibility of your business.

2020 Edition

By
FRANKIE J. FOSTER

MY FREE GIFT TO YOU

When you subscribe to my weekly email newsletter packed with information about websites for small businesses, you will receive for free a copy of *8 Costly and Common Website Mistakes Made by Small Businesses (with solutions)*.

This short, concise book shows business owners, managers and marketers some major website mistakes and how to correct them. You can download the book to your computer.

DOWNLOAD HERE
https://businesswebsitetips.com

THIS BOOK IS FOR...

Information in this book is directed to the personnel of small to medium-sized businesses, small start-up businesses and to the sole proprietor.

Business owners and personnel in a small business must wear many hats. The information in this book will ease the journey to produce a successful website.

Your Assignment: *Your company needs a new website or a redesign of an existing website. There is no professional website designer/developer on staff and you have been selected to determine the best avenue to produce a website.*

Your Qualifications: NONE

The information in this book helps you to jump right into the trenches and become competent to determine the best path to produce a business website that serves your clients and your business. You will learn the pros and cons for the various ways to have the website developed.

Reading this book can save you thousands of dollars and countless hours of time. (This book is approximately a two-hour read.) The end result will be a plan that will make the website successful online! That should certainly please everyone.

HERE'S YOUR SITUATION

You have an assignment to produce a website and you don't know where to begin.

Business owners, marketing managers and employees are overwhelmed with work in a small business. It is estimated there are over 28 million small businesses. Over three-quarters of small businesses are non-employers according to the SBA Office of Advocacy.

Problem: *It's been my experience as a web designer/developer that most small to medium-sized businesses don't have a website designer on staff.*

Whether someone is seeking to redesign an existing website or to develop a new website, most businesspeople have little or no experience or any familiarity with the elements, procedures and "dos" and "don'ts" of developing a website.

Solution: *This book will teach you how to proceed in obtaining a business website or a redesign of an existing site. You will understand the components of an effective website and their importance. You will be able to define your website's requirements and will be well-informed on the solutions to your website needs and goals.*

This book is a thorough guide to provide you with all the information you need to be qualified. You will be able to produce a successful website.

YOUR GOAL

The goal is to create an effective website that serves your company's needs at a reasonable cost.

Websites should be redesign approximately every 2-4 years to give your visitors and customers the best user experience.

The website's goals should focus on a clear message that you understand the needs of the visitors, have a solution and show them what actions to take. You want to have the website to be fast loading on mobile devices and to look great on all devices. The quality of the content must be high and the website must be optimized according to Google's algorithms.

If you are going to redesign an existing site, be specific with the reasons for your redesign, set goals for the redesign and decide the way to measure the before and after results.

If the business does not have a website, it must get one.

Though reasons for a website redesign will vary for every business, your basic website requirements are the same. The website must:

- Be attractive.
- Be mobile friendly.
- Load fast.
- Be organically optimized to rank on the first page of Google.
- Be responsive to all devices.
- Create a great user experience.
- Contain a clear message to solve a visitor's needs/wants.
- Have intuitive navigation.
- Have a direct call-to-action.
- Serve content to meet the visitor's needs.
- Serve your business.
- Be search engine friendly.
- Contain a lead capture form. (Without a lead capture form on your website, the digital content won't be capturing potential clients for your company. The purpose is to encourage visitors to sign up to receive a newsletter in exchange for a gift such as an ebook.) This is a great way to keep in touch and to develop new clients.

The site needs to be a complete package to inform, educate, serve and sell to your target audience. It is a company's most powerful information and sales tool. It is the hub of all your marketing and it is your strongest online presence. You want the website to be listed on the first page of Google and to convert visitors to customers.

Note: *Most people will judge the credibility of a company by its website.*

The information in this book will increase your knowledge and help you become educated on the website design process and hosting services. This information helps you determine the needs of your company's site and helps you select the best path to an end product that serves the company well.

Solutions Ahead

If you are the person to lead the company in the development or redesign of the website, the following information will help you determine the solution.

Press on...

SECTION 1

GET STARTED

1

DOMAIN NAME

The domain name, sometimes referred to as the URL or web address, is the address of the exact location of your website on the Internet. It is the name a visitor will key into the location or address bar of a browser to locate your website.

> *Note: A common mistake is to key in the exact web address in the search bar of a search engine instead of the location bar of the browser. Examples of web addresses: yahoo.com, google.com, thebytesite.com, or yourbusiness.com.*

You need to either locate or secure a domain name. The company may already have a website and/or domain name (URL) and you will need to track it down. If this is the case, be certain you know the registrar of the domain name and obtain the username and password to the registrar's website. Login in and make a note of the expiration date of the domain name and don't let the domain name expire.

> *Note: Be certain the email information at the registrar is current and the credit card information is current. You can set it to auto renew. If the credit*

card number and expiration date on the card is not current, the auto-renewal of the domain name won't process.

In most cases a registrar sends a notification to the email listed on the account many days before the expiration date of the domain name. If you do not renew by the expiration date, the domain name will expire. The registrar deactivates the domain name and it no longer points to the server hosting your website. DON'T LET THIS HAPPEN. Your life won't be easy if you do.

Though it is often referred to as buying a domain name (URL), we don't buy it. We pay for the right to use it. We can only be a "current registrant" of a domain name.

It is time for you to either locate the registrar of your existing domain name or to purchase the rights to a domain name from an authorized registrar.

If Your Website Already Exists on the Internet

If your company has a website, you will not need to register a domain name; someone previously registered it. There can be an exception: the site has a domain name that is a subdomain name of another site. Example: wix.com/yourcompanyname.

Still, you need to have your own domain name to establish credibility for the company. Example: yourcompanyname.com.

Note: Get control of the ownership of your company's domain name by having access to the registration account.

Reasons You Need Control of the Domain Name

Payments and Renewals: As an owner you must be in control of the domain name. The registration should be in your company's name with the contact information of someone in the company. Locate where the domain name is registered. Both you and/or the web designer will need the username and password for this registration.

Note: It is the owner's responsibility to renew the domain name and to pay the registrar. Payments to the registrars are made online by credit card and you must keep your credit card information updated in order for the automatic renewals to take place.

Directing Domain Name to Website Files: The domain name must point to the exact location of the website which resides on a host server in order for the website to be live.

If your site is not hosted at the same location as the registrar, then you or the web designer/developer will have to point the domain name to the proper host server.

When the site is published to the host server, either you or the web designer/developer must go to the registrar's site and provide the nameservers of the host server. Web developers/designers will either do this for you or tell you how to do it. Usually, they will do it.

Dismiss the Designer/Developer: Another reason you and your company will want the details of the domain registration is to dismiss your current web designer and to use the services of a new one. I have seen instances where some web designers become uncooperative when they are losing a client. This could be an instance when you want to change the usernames and passwords to the registrar account and the hosting account.

Problem: Often website designers will register a domain for their client. Too often, web designers will place the domain name registration in their own name or their business name—not the client's business name. You do not want this to happen.

Solution: Either register your own domain name or if the web designer/developer registers it for you, always insist they register your company name and information. Always possess the username and password for your account. As owner or company representative, be sure to change the username and password if you feel uneasy with those who have it.

Ways to Find Your Existing Domain Name

Inquire throughout your company to see if any records about the website or domain name are in the files. If all the information is there, you are fortunate.

If the complete records are not available, contact the former web designer for the information. This person should be able to tell you where it is registered and the username and password. The web designer would also know where an existing website it is being hosted.

If that is unsuccessful, visit the website www.whois.com. Place the domain name in the "Whois Lookup" box.

Sometimes the domain name's ownership information is hidden. If not hidden, the name of the owner (it should be your company, not a website designer's name) and the registrar is listed. In addition, they list the information for the hosting server. You may have to call the registrar of the domain name and prove ownership to secure the username and password if you cannot locate it in any other way.

If all this fails, ask the bookkeeper where they send payment to host the website. Call that company to get information.

Press on...

2

REGISTRAR

Acquire a Domain Name for a New Site

If you are setting up a new website, you need to purchase the right to use a domain name from an official registrar. Usually you can purchase it for one to ten years. Purchase it for two years or more—never for one year. A one-year registration throws up a flag to the search engines and indicates you might be a spammer.

Selecting a domain name is important. The name should reflect the brand and message of your business. It is best to keep it short, but more important than keeping it short is to keep it memorable.

By using an important keyword of your business in the domain name, the website will have an instant boost in the search engine rankings. Make the domain name readable. Avoid special symbols but it is all right to use the dash although dashes are unnecessary. Don't leave a space in the domain name.

The web address should be easy to say and spell.

When you select a domain name, put a lot of thought into it. Changing your domain name after your company's website is established on the Internet is risky and is a lot of trouble. It can lower your company's position in the search engine rankings and you will have to work to build it higher.

Search engines place value in having a keyword in the domain name. Here are some tips for selecting the name.

- Make certain it is your own domain name and not a subdomain name. You want to have www.yourdomainname.com not www.someoneelse.com/yourdomain.
- Select a .com extension. (75% of all websites have a .com extension) You can purchase the same in .biz, .net and other extensions.
- Select a name related to your core business.
- Consider using top keywords which describe your business.
- Make your domain name unique. Don't make it similar to an existing name.
- Make it easy to type, pronounce, spell, read and remember.
- It should not be like your competition's name.
- It should not violate a copyright.
- Avoid symbols, hyphens, dashes and numbers. You can use dashes but they are unnecessary. Search engines can now recognize separate words in your domain without dashes or hyphens. Dashes are not user friendly.
- To make it easier to read in your printed matter, capitalize the first letter of each word of your domain name if your domain name contains several words. Example: TheByteSite.Com. It will help people read it.

If you find that your preferred domain name is registered under all applicable suffixes, you need to get creative and think of another.

Keep in mind that the domain name can influence search engine results on Google and other search engines. Selecting a domain name that contains relevant search terms can increase its likelihood of appearing high in the search results.

> **Note:** *The domain name which contains a keyword will strengthen the positioning in search engine results. Example: dublinprintingservices.com*

Purchase the Domain Name

Domain names cost an average of $10.00-$12.00/year or if you are buying from an auction of domain names, you can pay hundreds or thousands of dollars.

Decide on a domain name and purchase it immediately. Purchase it for a minimum of two years or as long a period that makes you feel comfortable.

> **Note:** *Purchasing for one year can throw up a flag to the search engines that the domain is possibly used for spamming.*

Some hosting companies offer the cost of the domain registration free for the first year. It is best to check several companies to compare benefits and costs.

Ready to Proceed

At this point, you should have located all your existing site's information for the domain registration and where it is hosted.

Or if you do not have a site, determine the domain name for the new site and purchase it.

PRESS ON...

3

WEBSITE HOSTING

The web host is where all the website files will be placed on a server connected to the Internet. Now it is time to cover important factors that help you determine a good hosting service. Later, if working with a web developer/designer, you will determine the specific hosting features needed for your website.

SSL Certificate

The standard today is all websites should have an SSL (Secure Sockets Layer) Certificate which is a digital certificate that authenticates the identity of a website. It also encrypts information sent to the server using SSL technology. Encryption scrambles data into an undecipherable format and it can only be restored to a readable format with the proper decryption key.

If sites do not have the SSL Certificate, Google warns visitors with a tag that states a site is not secure. This warning may cause visitors to leave your website.

Google gives a small boost to the site's SEO ranking when it has the SSL Certificate. By installing the SSL, the site's speed improves and it provides a more secure experience for visitors.

Some hosting companies offer the certificate as a benefit included with your account and has no additional charge. Some charge for it.

> *Note: Small hosting firms may approach you to host your site with them. My experience has shown that many smaller firms lack security, lack features and have higher costs. In my 21 years of web design experience, only three sites I designed were hacked. Two of the clients had selected small, local servers managed by small firms without strong security.*

Important Features of Website Hosting Services:

- Outstanding 24/7 customer support
- Live technical support
- High running uptime
- Speed
- Backups
- Large amount of bandwidth
- Large amount of disk space
- Backend programming services
- Database support
- Unlimited number email boxes at no additional cost, includes many features, and has ease of set-up
- Spam protection
- Control panels
- Website statistics
- SSL Certificates
- Strong security
- Technical support

Press on...

SECTION 2

REVIEW YOUR EXISTING WEBSITE

4

REVIEW SITE'S STATISTICS AND ANALYTICS

If you have a website, you're not exactly starting with a blank page. Establish a benchmark.

- Review the website's statistics.
- Review the site's content and determine if it is still useful and up-to-date.
- Determine the site's position in the search engines for important keywords phrases.

Review Your Site's Statistics

If you have Google Analytics set up on the site, review the information. If you don't have Google Analytics, check with the host company to see if they have statistics. This information is valuable in measuring the success of the site, measuring the effectiveness of online advertising and is effective in determining the most visited and least visited areas of the site. These tools also can give a host of information and statistics such as referral traffic, bounce rate, average time on each page and on the site.

Analyze Traffic

By measuring the traffic to your site, you can compare it to the future growth of your new website or redesign. You can see how many visitors you have each day, month, and year. You not only see how many visitors who have been to the site, but the analytical software determines the number of visitors and the unique visitors. You may have 1,000 unique visitors and 1,500 visits in one month. This means 1,000 unique visitors visited a total of 1,500 times.

Beneficial and Effective Statistics

- How visitors are finding your site
- How long visitors remain on the site
- Entry page of visitor
- Exit page of visitor
- Tracks page views

How Does This Information Help You?

After reviewing the site's statistics, you might find that a lot of traffic is coming from social media, such as your Facebook page. You can immediately invest more of your online social media efforts on Facebook.

When you see which pages of your site are the most visited, you can use these pages to provide more information to the visitors.

If you have placed a video on the website and statistics show a high number of plays, consider adding more videos.

When you see how users interact with your website, you have identified the best opportunities for the growth of your online presence.

Measure Success of Marketing Campaigns

By reviewing and analyzing you website statistics, you can measure the success level of your marketing campaigns.

Visitor Information

You will see the amount of unique visitors to your site and the total amount of visits. Some visitors return several times.

Determine the Location of Visitors

If you have Google Analytics set up on your current site, you can look under "Visitors" menu to see the location demographics of your visitors.

Hits Versus Visitors

Many confuse hits with visitors. Each time a visitor lands on a web page, the page and all its graphics are loaded into the browser. The page, each graphic, video, and sound track count as a hit when it loads. For example, a webpage with one video and three photographs equals five hits but is is one page view.

Pages

Page statistics help you determine which pages are visited most often, how long people stay on a page and on which page visitors exit your site.

When you see a trend develop, that is a big sign that something is working or not working with that page. Trends show more than the actual numbers. You can determine which pages are more popular than others. You will also be able to see how long visitors are staying on each page.

Referrals

This section of statistics shows who is sending people to your website. It shows which search engines people use, the keywords and key phrases people use to find your site and shows other websites that are linked to your website.

PRESS ON...

RESEARCH YOUR SITE'S RANKING IN THE SEARCH ENGINES

The first step is to conduct the SEO audit of the major search engines which establishes a benchmark of ranking for different search phrases.

Search using the best keyword phrases that reflect your business, services or products. Think like a potential client and use keyword phrases they would use.

This is a great way to measure progress or decline after the new website is designed. Keep a record of your results. It is wise to perform this research regularly.

October, 2019 Top Search Engines According Net MarketShare

- Google - 71.86% World Market
- Baidu (China) - 15.54% World Market
- Bing - 7.7% World Market
- Yahoo - 4.0% World Market

PRESS ON...

6

REVIEW LEADS AND SALES GENERATED BY CURRENT SITE

Discovering the leads and sales generated by the current website can be difficult to gather unless you or someone in your company has recorded the website's sales leads and sales results. If they have kept no written record, try to determine this information as best as you can.

If your company has a weakness in tracking leads and sales, then it is time to set a plan in place.

Regardless of your type of business, the website can always generate leads which will give you an opportunity to convert them into sales.

Visitors may come to your site with no intention of buying; they may come to your site simply to research. You want to provide a lot of information about your products and services.

Press On...

SECTION 3

DECIDE HOW TO BUILD THE NEW WEBSITE

HOW SHOULD YOU BUILD THE NEW WEBSITE?

Should you use an online build-it-yourself website design platform or hire a professional designer/developer?

During the middle 90s when commercial websites were relatively new, it was better to be on the web with any kind of website than to have no website at all. By the end of the 90s and the start of 2000, there was a dot-com boom and the competition began for ranking on the first page of search engine results.

To meet your company's website needs, you might ask, "Why not use an online build-it-yourself website where you drag-and-drop elements to create your own website?" Many of these cloud-based web hosting companies offer pre-built templates besides the drag-and-drop technologies. Some build-it-yourself sites suggest you can create your website with a few clicks and save hundreds to thousands of dollars. That may be true for the short term, but let's look at the upside and downside of this method which allows you to make a website with no knowledge of copywriting, presentation, user-experience, organic optimization or coding.

If you are on a limited budget and you don't know how to code, design or write for a website, you might consider the idea to do it yourself with one of the drag-and-drop online website builder sites. Should you use one?

If you are a small, start-up business and with no funds, maybe using a website builder is the only way to have an online presence.

> *Note: Only in a few situations it might be better to have a do-it-yourself website than to have no website at all. But a poorly designed, structured and poorly written website will cost your company more money by the loss of trust, visitors, buyers, your reputation and income.*

> *Caution: An unattractive website, a confusing appearance, weak content, lots of clutter, slow loading and bad design will drive visitors away. That will cost your business money.*

Your website is an important investment. It gives website users a crucial first impression of your company. It will cost you the loss of clients and income if you have a website a poor appearance and one with poor performance. The website's purpose is to generate leads, sales and revenue for your company, not to lose clients and income.

Before we begin the pros and con of each, remember that any website that is simply placed online and then forgotten will become ineffective.

Websites need:

- To be current with technology.
- To be updated with new content frequently.
- To be incorporated in your strategic marketing plan.

Let's weigh the advantages and disadvantages of hiring a professional or attempting to do it yourself.

. . .

PRESS ON...

PROS OF A BUILD-IT-YOURSELF WEBSITE BUILDER

The build-it-yourself site platform furnishes you with a large selection of professionally designed templates from which to choose. There are many companies offering these builders and pre-built templates.

- Build-it-yourself companies state you can build your site in a short time.
- Plans start free and go higher.
- These websites appear to be an easy and inexpensive business solution.
- You don't need to have knowledge of code or skills to design graphics.
- Builders offer a wide range of features.
- They provide you with stock photographs and icons.
- They offer decent designs and templates.
- Low, up-front cost is an attractive feature.
- Includes hosting.
- Often includes a free SSL certificate.
- You will have no delays in updating.

- You can use your own domain name. (May add an extra cost.)
- Offers some SEO plans.
- Includes image editor.
- Includes social icons.

PRESS ON...

CONS OF A BUILD-IT-YOURSELF WEBSITE BUILDER

Becomes an Indecisive Log Jam

You create many headaches and problems when you try to complete one of these do-it-yourself sites. Instead of building your website in a short time, it can eat up hours of your time experimenting with the settings, different menus and creating content.

Requires Professional Knowledge of Copywriting

Writing the content becomes difficult even for someone educated in another field instead of copywriting. This will be your biggest hurdle. It takes time to organize and professional knowledge of copywriting to write and structure compelling content that converts your visitors to clients.

A business owner or employee has duties of dealing with the operation or production in the business. It is difficult to find the time to complete the site and to learn all the ins and outs of a successful website.

My most recent experiences relate to a public relations company and an education consultant for secondary schools and colleges. Both were stuck for months (over 12 months) trying to decide on the content for their sites and how to use the builder.

One person completed the site, and the other abandoned the project. The site that was completed does not rank on either the first or second page of Google. When viewing the site, it is difficult to determine the purpose of the website.

Lacks Customized Appearance

You need an attractive website and the website builder can provide that. A downside is many other people are using the same pre-built template and photographs you are using. That does not speak well for the seriousness of your business nor does it contribute to the success of your business.

Doesn't Reflect Company's Branding

Using a template can interfere with the continuity of your company's branding. Your goal is to have a website that continues the branding of your company. It is not your goal to create a website that looks the same as other business websites. Your goal is to make your business stand out by reflecting it brand.

Loss of Income

If you are taking your time away from running your business, you are not producing income.

When an employee is assigned to build the website, compute the amount of hours spent and multiply that times their hourly salary. It will be an astonishing amount and you will still have an amateur website.

Random Design and Content Placement

You will place your content at random on web pages unless you take the time to study human behavior and engagement on websites.

Site Can't be Moved

Many on the websites on the build-it-yourself platforms don't allow you to migrate the site to another server. If you become dissatisfied with the company, you can leave them but not with your website. If you can't move your website to another platform, you really don't own it.

Lack of Phone Technical Support

Most of the build-it-yourself website platforms don't have any phone technical support. The support they offer is generic and often inaccurate.

PRESS ON...

10
WHAT SHOULD YOU DO?

If you are a hobbyist, these website builders are right for you. If you need a quick website for a party or an event, a website builder is fine and is a small investment. Some are free but the builder company might place advertisements on your website.

If you need a website for a new business or an existing business, using a build-it-yourself website builder can cause the loss of time and money for your business but, most important, can damage the reputation of your business.

> *Note: The website is the most important piece of marketing collateral for your company.*

Most business owners don't understand what comprises the best online presence. Most people may be experts in their own business field but not in content writing, graphic design, search engine optimization, technical structure of a website, digital marketing or how to provide a great user experience for the visitor. A great user experience is an important factor to keep your visitor interested.

Google places high importance of user experience in the ranking of websites.

Using the drag and build platforms may give an attractive website but that is only a beginning to success. The website may also look like a lot of other company sites and may lack crucial elements of success.

Load Speed of a Website Is Critical

Google: 53% of mobile users abandon sites that take over three seconds to load.

This is important. Most people are accessing the Internet through mobile devices and if your site doesn't load quickly, you lose visitors.

Visitors expect a site to load within two seconds. If not, they become subconsciously irritated and more impatient. At three seconds, you lose 53% of your audience. With each additional second, the loss is higher.

Your site needs to be fast loading, professionally written and presented to attract and keep the attention of your visitors. The site should be able to convert visitors into clients. It should be organically optimized to rank high in the search engine results.

You won't know how to present content effectively unless you take the time to study human behavior on a website.

The site must present content to tell the visitor what you have, how it can solve their problems and the design must guide them to a call of action. You have approximately two or three seconds to keep a visitor once they open the site.

Search Engine Optimization

Most website builders have poor search engine optimization and do not offer the tools to optimize the website. A good website designer/developer can offer a great advantage with keyword research and website optimization.

If you have used the drag-and-drop builder, do you know how to test your new site on Google's test site to discover how long the website takes to load?

Do you know how to make the site search engine friendly?

Google presents its search results from a mobile perspective. Are you able to make certain the site loads on a 3G network within three to five seconds?

Your site's performance is to keep and inform visitors, improve conversions, and to give both users and your company complete success.

When you test your site, be sure you are using the test Google provides. The site is https://www.thinkwithgoogle.com/feature/testmysite. They test on both the 3G and 4G networks. Another place to check your website is https://gtmetrix.com. It shows you how your site performs; it reveals why it is slow and provides optimizations solutions.

Below are some core website features and metrics you should check with browser tools. The list is probably overwhelming and boring to the non-developer but they are critical for creating a successful website.

- Load time performance on 3G and 4G networks
- Timeline events for loading and parsing resources and memory usage
- Total page weight and the number of files
- Number and weight of JavaScript files
- Any particularly large individual JavaScript files (over 100KB)
- Total number and weight of image files

- Any particularly large individual image files
- Image formats—PNGs that could be JPEGs or SVGs?
- Whether responsive image techniques (such as srcset) are used
- HTML file size
- Total number and weight of CSS files
- Unused CSS
- Problematic usage of other assets such as web fonts (including icon fonts).
- DevTools timeline for anything that blocks page load.

Sounds a little overwhelming? Sorry! It is overwhelming to the non-designer or non-developer but all the above information is critical to the success of a website.

More Serious Drawbacks of the Build-It-Yourself Sites

Below is a list of some limitations, considerations and dangers of using the drag-and-drop builders:

- Some website building companies don't allow you to use your own domain name. A business cannot accept this.
- If the business wants credibility and respect, a free and cheap template is not a proper representation of your company. It can look like other websites which use the same graphics. Unless you replace the graphics, (they need to be quality, relevant and optimized graphics) other sites using the same template will look like yours.
- If you customize one of these templates, you need knowledge, design skills and software to create, size and output your own graphics. You need to optimize the graphics. Mistakes made here can ruin both the appearance and performance of the site. Low quality graphics give your business a bad image.
- Most business owners/employees don't know how to create

an attractive graphic or know how to write a web page's content to make a site convert a visitor to a client.

- Can you organize and present a well-designed page with content organized so the visitors can determine if this site is for them?
- Some website builders don't allow a way to insert Google Analytics code. (Google Analytics is a free digital analytics tool. It has solutions available to measure and understand web traffic and behavior. It can provide key insights to your marketing. The information from Google Analytics helps businesses understand the source of the traffic and if media campaigns are performing well.)
- Several website builders create sites heavy with code and you can't access the proper files to optimize and minify them.
- If you register a domain name with a website builder company, it can be **difficult** to get control of it to point it to the new website on another server.
- Users report (and I have experienced it) that website builder companies lack adequate customer service. Most have no phone number.
- A cheap-looking, poorly written website will cost you loss of income.
- Not being found in the search engines will cost you loss of income.

UNLESS you know how to design, create unique graphics, develop the information architecture, write a website that will attract your visitor's attention and load quickly on mobile devices, don't use the build-it-yourself platform for your business website.

Your site needs to take your visitors on an organized experience through the website. It should give them a logical path that recognizes and solves their needs and makes them want to take an action to read, to contact you or to purchase your products and/or services.

If you are serious about your business, don't jeopardize its success with an inferior site.

Solution

Your website is the hub of your online presence and marketing. It is the first impression of your business for most potential clients. Make it a great first impression.

Since your website is for commercial intent, hire a professional website designer/developer. You don't have to have a large site. Start small and grow the site.

With my experience of designing and developing websites for clients, quite a few of my clients previously tried the "do-it-yourself" platforms before seeking my professional website services. These clients experienced various difficulties and had little success with building their own website on these platforms. They lacked the time and knowledge to make the website high quality and the site did not reflect the high quality of their businesses.

If you want to see a return on your website and earn respect and credibility from potential clients, hire a professional website designer/developer. The cost of a professionally designed website is a sound investment.

PRESS ON...

11

REASONS TO HIRE A PROFESSIONAL

Original Design

You will have an original and unique design if you hire a professional website designer/developer. You will receive a high quality, optimized website.

A professional designer/developer's job is to understand website design's best practices, the use of fonts, colors and balance. They design the user interface, content and architecture to flow toward needs of your visitors. All these factors contribute to generating leads, conversions and sales.

Website Optimization and Usability

Without an optimized site structure, images and content, visitors won't find the site. If your website doesn't provide a great visual design and user experience, the site won't be a success.

Optimized for Search Engine (SEO)

A professional has knowledge of the search engine optimization elements for the construction of the website. Both the technical design, visual design and user experience are crucial to the success of a website. You must have an attractive, well-designed website which loads quickly and contains clear navigation. The content should spark the interest of the visitor and encourage the visitor to a call-to-action.

A professional who works in design and development and has knowledge of SEO can increase your website's chances of appearing high in search engine page results. The higher you can rank in the organic search engine results, the more opportunity you have to bring in new clients.

Visual Experience

Web users judge a company on their first impression of how fast the page loads, on the information they need and on the visual impact and design of your website.

Since most website visitors access the Internet via their mobile devices, you must make certain the business website is responsive and looks good on a smartphone, desktop, laptop and tablet.

Copywriting

Visit a few websites and note what is on the first screen of the site. How many of them are touting their years in business and the awards they have won? Visitors don't come to you website to see how many years you have been business or to read your mission statement. Nobody is coming to a website for any other reason than for themselves. Visitors won't browse your website for several minutes to find what they want. You have only two or three-seconds to show them you have what they want and need. If the website is complicated and cluttered, they are gone!

The content on a website should steer the visitors where you want them to go. Unless you are an educated writer for websites, I suggest you hire a professional.

A beautifully designed and optimized website is just the start of success. Without the elements of great copywriting, a gorgeous website will fail. The copy needs to attract the visitor, address the needs of the visitor and provide a solution. Effective copywriting is essential for a website's success and to be found on Google's first page.

Do you know how people read online? Do you know where people spend most of their time on the home page? Do you know the results of eye-tracking tests? Website professionals do. They have researched and studied to understand website user behavior. With research, they know the most common paths and behaviors of visitors on a website.

Professional copywriters know to research and focus on keywords with high conversion rates.

User Experience

An experienced website professional knows the components that create an impactful visual experience and a successful user experience.

Press on...

SECTION 4

PREPARATION FOR WEBSITE DEVELOPMENT WITH A
PROFESSIONAL DESIGNER/DEVELOPER

12

GATHER CONTENT FOR THE WEBSITE

Before contacting a professional website developer/designer, it is time to determine the content for the website.

Gathering information for your website is probably the most difficult task you must perform. Often it is the biggest delay in completing most websites.

Don't delay this chore but discipline yourself to complete it quickly. A few suggestions and ideas will help with the entire process of gathering and organizing the content and information.

> *Note: If you don't dedicate the time for this task, the website will come to a standstill.*

A good web designer/developer won't quote or start a project until they see all the content and understand your company's needs. They can give you an accurate quote when they know all the materials you want to include on the website. They can't create the design and presentation or organize the site's content without seeing all of it.

Note: Trying to design the website without all the content is like trying to complete a jigsaw puzzle without all the pieces. Without the content, the web designer/developer won't be able to give you an accurate quote for the work.

Who knows the most about your customers or their needs? The sales staff knows!

Your sales staff's insight into customers' needs is invaluable. Customers want solutions to their problems and need new and innovative solutions. Information from the sales staff will be a great contribution to your website's content.

Speak to the sales personnel. A good salesperson knows the questions clients frequently ask. They see the client's needs and how the client responds to your company's products and information.

Sources for information (suggested but not limited to):

- Company brochures
- Product brochures
- Product/services lists with descriptions
- Publication articles
- News articles about your business
- Press releases
- Recent advertising campaigns
- Posters
- Videos
- All printed materials
- Logos
- Sales brochures
- Top quality photographs (products, facility, company founder/personnel)
- Customer testimonials
- Awards and recognitions
- Association memberships

- Company history
- Current news
- Interviews
- Existing website

When you have all your information gathered, it is time to determine your budget.

Determine Your Budget

It is time to realize how much a website might cost and how to determine a budget.

> *Note: If you don't have a website, you are losing business to those who do. If you have a poorly designed, ugly, cluttered website, you are losing business to those who have a professional-looking website. Remember, the website is the hub of your marketing.*

The Value of Your Site

This is the first impression many will have of your business. A well-designed site will provide credibility to your business. A well-written and presented website will keep your visitors engaged and make it easy for them to move about the site to see if your business offers what they need.

- This is not the place to cut costs, but it is a place to be a smart shopper for a qualified website designer/developer.
- Your website is an investment.
- The website is a tool to provide customers with the exact information they are seeking.
- The website will be representation of your company's quality.

A well-design, professional looking website provides a cost effective marketing tool that can reach unlimited visitors. It is an instant way a potential client can research your services and products. The site can be the first impression on many potential clients and it will create a lasting impression.

A properly designed site will provide credibility to your business.

- Compare the cost of newspaper or magazine ads to a website on a monthly basis. The website wins by a large financial margin.
- When you compare the viewership for a print ad to the viewership of a website, the potential market you can reach with the website is larger and is a more cost effective way to promote your business.
- A website is easy to change and update unlike the company's printed materials.
- The website is a product where you can build an email list to stay in contact with customers or potential customers.
- You can use the website to distribute printed or digital materials or to educate visitors with videos. (Be sure to distribute to them by collecting their email addresses with permission to send further information.)

It you want to be perceived as a serious business, you must have a professional-looking website. Potential buyers search for information online before purchasing at a brick and mortar stores.

The Internet creates a level playing field. A well-designed, attractive website can portray as professional an image as any large company can portray.

Use a professional web designer/developer to create your website. Do not use some amateur, relative or some inexperienced person who has no knowledge on how to portray a business image or to create a website properly.

Factors That Influence Website Design Costs

Potential clients often ask a website designer, "How much does a website cost?" I equate that question to "How much does a car cost?" This comparison usually helps the caller understand there are many variables to consider when buying a car and the same applies for buying a website.

A car can cost from under $8,000 to over $1,000,000. The range of cost for a website can vary the same way. It is a wide range.

Before a website designer can estimate costs for you, you need to explain your objectives, goals and content for the website.

Whoever determines the budget for the company should be able to provide you with an estimate of funds available for the website project.

It is best to meet with several designers to discuss the website. Upon hearing your objectives and goals and viewing the content, they will give recommendations that will be invaluable.

The cost of the site will depend on the amount of content you have and the features you need and want.

Typical price ranges for websites:

- Less than $1,200
- $1,200 - $2,300
- $2,300 - $5,000
- $5,000+

Factors that influence cost:

- Amount of content
- Type of content to be displayed
- Photo galleries
- Copywriting

- Special functions
- Special programming needed for special functions
- Content management system
- Training with a user guide for the content management system
- Contact forms
- E-commerce
- Interactive database site
- A blog
- Additional security (especially needed for WordPress sites)
- A way to collect email addresses to send your e-newsletter
- Forms or documents you may want your visitor to download.
- Set up of social websites
- Website updates
- Secure website with an SSL certificate.
- Set up Google Analytics

Now it is time to find the right website designer/developer.

Press on...

13

FINAL THOUGHTS BEFORE APPROACHING A WEBSITE DESIGNER/DEVELOPER

Define the Business Objectives of the Website for the Visitors You Want to Attract

When you speak with your website designer/developer, be prepared to discuss and define the customers you want to attract to your website and the action you want them to take.

You are not looking for large numbers of visitors—just all visitors interested in your products and services. You need to inform customers about all your products or services. Remember, you only have a few seconds to keep their attention, solve their problems and to prompt them to take a call-to-action.

One visitor who needs and wants your products or services is invaluable. Twenty visitors who have no need for your products or services are worthless.

Perhaps your business supplies ice cream makers to ice cream plants and restaurants. You are not looking for visitors who want to purchase ice cream. Those visitors are not potential customers. You are looking for visitors who make ice cream on a large scale.

Direct the site's information to your specific audience. It must be well organized and thorough. It is valuable to have an experienced copywriter write for your website.

Keep in mind when someone writes content for your site, they must write for the visitor. They are not writing for the company or for the search engines but for the visitor. Understand the needs of your customer and show how your products and services meet those needs. Show how your products or services can make the visitor's life or business easier.

Present unique identifiers about your company, products, and services and define what sets you apart from others. Tell the visitor how your services or products will benefit them.

If you place massive information on your website, it must be organized and presented so your visitor can quickly find what they need. People browse and scan a web page to find the information. That is why your site's information must be formatted into clear and coherent short blocks of text with descriptive headers. People won't read large blocks of text.

PRESS ON...

SECTION 5

FIND THE RIGHT WEBSITE DESIGNER/DEVELOPER

14
TIME TO START

Arm yourself with your content, budget and questions and set off on this journey.

It is time to locate a web designer/developer to help you write and present the company's information in a professional, logical, attractive, effective, optimized, fast loading, easy to navigate website that is responsive to all devices. Whew!

Remember, your visitors need a site that is inviting, responsive, interesting and intuitive. Visitors will leave the site quickly if they don't get what they need or if they don't know what to do.

Google expects your site to be responsive and to load quickly and you want the website to convert visitors to customers.

Website Designer or Website Developer?

Why look for a website designer/developer? Why not look for just a website designer or only a website developer?

The main strength of a website designer is the visual creativity and careful planning while the main strength of a website developer is the programming to implement the design.

A website designer/developer will offer you the combined package. This simplifies the process when you find someone who has both design and development skills. If you are fortunate, you will find a website designer/developer who has been trained in copywriting for websites. If you don't find that combination, the company you select should have available resources to provide all areas of the website's development.

It is your decision whether you hire a sole proprietor business, a mid-size company or a large company.

Consider someone who has:

- Great communication skills to explain their process.
- Creative design skills.
- Programming skills.
- Responsive design knowledge.
- Copywriting skills.
- Search engine optimization knowledge.
- User experience design.
- A portfolio of a variety of websites.
- References.

Referral

A referral is one of the best ways to find a website designer/developer. If you know someone with a great website (business associates, suppliers, local chamber of commerce or friends), ask for the name of the company or individual who designed and developed their site. In fact, ask several people for referrals.

Online Searches

A search online will render a large list of designer/developers in your area. It is still nice to have a referral.

Regardless where you find your referrals, be sure to visit their websites to see the quality and style of their work.

PRESS ON...

15

INTERVIEWS AND SELECTION

What to Expect from a Designer/Developer?

A good designer/developer:

- Knows your site must respond to all devices.
- Knows the main objective of a website is have a clear message that meets the visitor's needs and to draw a response from the visitor.
- Knows the site must create trust in your company.
- Can produce the site within your budget.
- Is a good communicator and will listen to you; will assess your needs and provide both feedback and suggestions.
- Can grasp the concept of your company and apply creativity to the design of the site which follows your company's brand.
- Will create a site unique in its appearance and will set your company apart from its competitors.
- Knows that you have only a few seconds to capture the visitor's attention and to show your company's value.
- Is someone who understands copywriting for the website;

understands marketing and visitor conversions to help optimize the design of your site.

- Knows visitors have short attention spans and you will get better results with short blocks of text with headings, white space, photographs, artwork and videos. (Don't use with large blocks of text. Use plenty of white space.)
- Can portray your company, products and service to website visitors to get them to respond in the way you want.
- Knows that simplicity is important.
- Knows ease-of-use will keep your visitors engaged on the site.
- Will build your site to meet the needs of both your visitor and search engine requirements.
- Will recommend you set up Google Analytics for your site in your own account—not their account.

When Meeting with a Website Designer/Developer

You need to:

- State the range of your budget.
- Discuss your needs for the project.
- State the main objective of the website. Perhaps it is to generate more sales, subscribers, traffic.
- Determine if you need a content management system (CMS). If you need a large amount of content changed on a regular basis, consider a CMS. My observation has been that clients don't frequently change content enough to make the cost of the CMS a value to them. Measure the difference in cost to install a content management system to the cost of your web designer performing the updates. If you plan to add a blog on your website, you will need the CMS.
- Make certain your web developer includes the organic SEO elements to your site—meta title, meta description, site map designed for Google, xml site map...

- Ask to see sites designed by the designer/developer.
- Request references.
- Make certain website design is their full-time career.
- Ask about their site building process.
- Ask who will perform the work.
- Ask how long they have been creating websites.
- Ask about their qualification for writing website copy.
- Evaluate their work for appearance and determine if they can meet your site's needs.
- Make certain you feel comfortable in understanding the designer/developer especially when discussing the technical issues of the site's design?
- Explain how you want your business to be perceived. You want to get your vision communicated clearly to the designer.
- Make certain your site will be organically optimized for the search engines.
- Expect a written quote and contract which lists all the services you will receive.
- Request several designs from which to choose.
- Establish a production timeline.
- Establish the payment schedule.
- Establish how your site will be backed-up.
- Establish who will set up Google Analytics.

Meet with Several Website Designer/Developers

After interviewing and reading the proposals of several website designer/developers, select the one you feel best meets your requirements.

PRESS ON...

16

AFTER YOU SELECT YOUR WEBSITE DESIGNER/DEVELOPER

Schedule A Meeting

Schedule a meeting to:

- Define the contract.
- Work with the company to determine a timeline for the different phases of the site's development from the moment you deliver all content to the designer until the publishing of the site online.
- Establish a financial payment schedule. A reputable company will want a portion of the payment to initiate the project and will specify when the balance will be due.
- Itemize a list of the content and schedule the date for delivering all your content to the designer/developer.
- Obtain the designer/developer contact information—phone number, address and email address.
- If the designer/developer is going to register your domain name, make certain that the domain name is registered in your company's name and that you receive the registrar's website address with the username and password. Learn

how you keep your payment data current and how to renew the domain with the registrar.

- Ask how your site will be organically designed and optimized for the search engines.
- You want the site to load quickly on mobile and desktop devices.
- Make certain that the site will be responsive to all devices and will look good on all devices—desktop, tablets and phones.
- Determine which areas of the site will need to be frequently updated and determine if a content management system is needed. If it is needed, determine the details.
- Determine the specific CTAs (Call-to-Actions) that should be on every page of your website. The CTA should be related to the action you want the visitor to take.

PRESS ON...

17

DELIVER CONTENT TO WEBSITE DESIGNER/DEVELOPER

It is time to present all the materials you gathered to the website designer/developer. This should include all brochures, photographs, videos, press releases, current newsletters, company background/history and client endorsements. All content should be relevant to the business.

The designer/developer should review the materials, have copy prepared for the website, create the structure and graphics for the content and add the proper calls-to-action.

Visitors don't read a web page the same as they read printed material. Web visitors scan. They read the headings, small blocks of text and bulleted lists to see if the content applies to their needs. If they can't find information related to their needs quickly, they leave your site.

Discuss the Site's Appearance and Performance

User Experience (UX) - Considered Important by Google - The user experience (UX) is important and a critical factor. Google considers the UX as a vital input to their search algorithms to rank high and to maintain a high rank in their search engine results. Important factors that provide a successful UX are the site's load speed, ease of navigation, relevant content, content that leads a visitor to take action and mobile responsiveness.

Responsive Design - More people access the Internet from their mobile devices than from their desktop systems. Because of this, your site must be responsive to mobile devices and to the desktops and laptops.

In the past separate sites were designed—one for desktops and laptops and one for mobile devices. Each had its own domain name. Today, there is seldom a need to create a separate website for mobile.

A responsive website can be designed to fit the needs of all device users. Separate sites create a larger cost and are time consuming to maintain. One responsive website design is the solution which serves all the devices. It saves you time and money.

Responsive websites serve the same information to both desktop and mobile devices. It simply rearranges and resizes the content depending on the device calling up the website.

Another benefit of having only one responsive website is it makes the search engines happy. Having multiple sites makes it hard for the search engines. Having just one website with one domain name makes it simpler for the search engines to crawl and rank the site.

Website Speed is Critical

Google expects a site to load in five seconds on the 3G network. Of course, it will be much faster on newer networks.

Google crawls the web from a mobile browser view. If a site isn't optimized for mobile, its rankings can plummet. In other words, mobile-friendly should be your top priority now, if it hasn't been before.

Long load times increase the number of visitors leaving the website before it loads.

Relevant Content - Vital to Visitors and Google

Google's intent is to show results that accurately answer the search queries of Internet users.

The website should provide relevant, compelling content to the visitors you want to attract. This is one of the most critical factors in keeping the visitors on the site.

With a fast load time for the website, the visitors can evaluate it quickly. The home page content should show them what your site is about, what it offers them and show an action you want them to take.

Branding

As the most important component of a company's online presence, the website should reflect accurately and effectively your company's brand identity. The elements of the site, logos, photographs, colors, text, design and navigation, need to be an accurate representation.

Credibility - Good for Visitors and Helps Rank Higher in Google

- Show your visitors your website is a valuable tool for them.
- Keep the website updated with current news about your company's products/services.
- Show icons of your social media sites.
- List some of your clients.
- List company awards and recognitions.
- Show client reviews.

Properly displayed, these items show credibility for the company.

Custom Design

By having it custom designed, the website should match your brand by using artwork and photography that represents your company.

Using a pre-designed theme that others are using can be spotted by savvy consumers. Again, this weakens the credibility and professionalism of a company.

Logo

A logo is an important part of a company's identity—the most visual element of your business. Based on studies, visitors expect the logo to be in the upper left of the website and on all interior pages.

Photographs and images

Scientists have proven that people remember visuals better than text.

The photographs used on the site must be high quality. Quality photographs and artwork, along with professionally written copy, will have an important impact on your visitors and the amount of time they stay on the site.

Appealing visuals contribute to the visitor's pleasurable experience. The lack of quality on a website can show the lack of seriousness of your business and harm its credibility. It can't be stressed too much that quality photographs and graphics are essential for the success of your website.

Design Elements

Other elements critical to the appearance of the site follows:

- Colors
- Fonts

- Art elements
- Call-to-action buttons

Interactions with Visitors - Vital to Visitors and Google

Include areas which allow your target audience to interact with your site. Below are some examples you might want to include:

- Subscription box allowing visitors to receive your newsletter. This provides a lead generator for your business. Be sure to reward them with a gift for subscribing.
- Call-to-action buttons
- Gallery to showcase your products and business
- Search box to help locate information on the site
- Frequently asked questions (FAQ)
- Form for contacting your business
- Live chat for online information and help
- Comment area
- Google map
- Customer reviews
- Videos

Press on...

18

TIME TO REVIEW SAMPLE WEBSITES

When you select the new website design, select the design which accurately represents your business and best serves your potential client.

The new design will be the first impression of the business for many visitors. If it is messy, confusing, slow and unattractive, visitors will leave.

The first screen of your website is the most important.

They often refer to the first screen as "above the fold." This is the screen people see when they land on your website before they scroll down the page.

The first screen should briefly:

- Identify a need or desire of the client.
- State how you can solve their need.
- Have a clear call-to-action. (Also include the call-to-action in the navigation at the top right of the page.)

Can visitors quickly see what your company does and how it will help them?

Your message should be clear and concise.

Is the text formatted in a way to make the text easy to scan?

Internet users skim through the content instead of reading. Does your site offer plenty of white space and have headings, sub-headings, short paragraphs, bulleted lists to help readers navigate through the page to find what they need?

Does the site look great on mobile?

Preview the site and its functions on phones, tablets, laptops and desktops.

Do the graphics look attractive and interesting?

Photographs and graphics help visitors find interest and ease in reading the page.

> *Note: You have one chance to make a first impression on your visitor. Select your new design wisely!*

Decision Time

Make the selection for your new design from the samples!

PRESS ON...

19

REVIEW BEFORE LAUNCH

Most designers will place the website on a staging server where you can review the content and test most of the functions of the site.

Have several people in your company help you review the website.

Pre-Launch Checklist

- Is the website visually appealing?
- Is the navigation clear and easy to understand?
- Is there a clear message to visitors about something they need and how your company can meet their needs?
- Are there call-to-action buttons?
- Does the website load within five seconds on a 3G network?
- Is the website is responsive?
- Does the website look good on all devices?
- Is your business name and address in text (as opposed to a graphic)?
- Verify phone number, address, hours of operation and contact information on all pages.
- Does it include client testimonials?
- Are associations, awards and recognitions included?

- Includes links to your social pages?
- No auto-play of videos or audios is enabled.
- Social icons should not be at the top of a website. No need to take visitors away from the site as soon as they arrive.
- Make sure all fonts are easy to read.
- Proofread content for accuracy.
- Check grammar, punctuation, and spelling.
- Check site's navigational links.
- Is content scannable?
- Are links noticeable?
- Check internal page links to make certain they go where intended.
- Check links to external sites to ensure they open in new browser windows and go where intended.
- Make certain all images (except background images) have alt tags.
- Make certain the site logo links to the home page. This is a common practice.
- Confirm with the designer/developer that the site is backed up. You don't want to lose anything now or even later.
- If the designer/developer is designing it on his own system, make sure he backs it up on his system and can restore the site should an online catastrophe occur.
- The host server should have capabilities for backing up a website. Sometime there may be a fee for it but it is well worth the cost.

Review These Items with the Website Designer

Page Meta Title

Definitely, this is one of the most important elements of a web page. The title appears in the top bar of the browser.

This should be a concise description of the page's content. Use important keywords near the beginning of the title.

Length: Google's title tag recommended length is 70–71 characters. The title appears in the search engine results and should have an accurate reflection of your web page. Typically, Google displays the first **50–60 characters** of the title tag.

Page Meta Description

Google suggests using 160 characters for the meta description.

> **Note:** *Make certain both meta titles and descriptions are in place at launch time because search engine may find and index the site quickly.*

Optimized Headings (H-1 through H-6) and Content

The H-1 heading should be at the top of the page and contain the most important content and keywords. There should only be one H-1. As the importance of the information decreases, the headings should follow H-2 through H-6. If your information has a content of equal importance, it won't hurt the site to repeat the H-2 heading several times if needed.

Again, the most important information always goes at the top of the page and the rest of the information should appear according to its relevancy.

The longer the keyword rich content, the higher it will rank in the search engine results.

Remember, high quality writing, focused on the information your visitor needs, will always rank well in the search engine results. Be sure to use targeted keywords in your content. Be careful not to repeat them too often. It makes your writing look contrived. An honest approach to writing for the reader is the best approach.

Page Speed

Page speed is critical. Most visitors will wait about three seconds for a webpage. After three seconds, half of your visitors will leave. Page load time is a major factor in Google's ranking algorithm.

ALT Tags

An ALT tag is used to describe an image and what it represents. These tags benefit the visually impaired users who use screen readers when browsing. Also, they benefit those who surf the web with images turned off or users who have text-only browsers. Alt tags should describe what is in the image.

Images

Images need to be optimized to remove all unnecessary data. A professional website designer/developer will know to optimize them without loss of quality. Just verify this with your designer.

Alt tags need to be added for each image. Alt tags have a strong correlation with Google SEO rankings, so be certain to add a descriptive alt tag containing keywords when you have images and videos on your pages. Again, verify these with the designer.

Google Analytics Set Up

Google Analytics collects data about the usage of your website. It is a free tool and you can monitor the user activity on the website.

Though it only takes a few minutes to set up the account, discuss whether you want the designer/developer to set it up or if this is something you want to do. If the designer/developer sets up the account, make certain it is in the company's name and they provide you with the username and address.

After the account has been established, there is a snippet of code that needs to be added to each page. Google Analytics processes the site's data and information. A few metrics are listed below:

- The number of visitors
- The total time a user spends on your site
- The time a user spends on each page and the order they visit those pages

- Internal links clicked (based on the URL of the next page view)
- The geographic location of the user
- Browser and operating system used to view the website
- Screen size and whether Flash or Java is installed
- The referring site

Evaluate the Written Content

Your website's content is key to keeping a visitor engaged. Great copywriting is an absolute essential to the success of your website. The quality of your copy will determine the rise of your brand. Securing a skilled copywriter is, these days, mandatory.

- Content must recognize the problems the visitor has without your product/service.
- Content must give a vision of the future if the visitor uses your product/service.
- Your information shows how you can solve the problems.
- People will rely on a website that inspires confidence.

PRESS ON...

LAUNCH THE WEBSITE

Launch Day

Your designer/developer may suggest the best time to launch the site. Ensure that it is a day that will least impact your business.

Initially, there should be a soft-launch—a launch without announcements, publicity or marketing. This gives you time to verify there are no issues.

Select a few trusted users to help test for you. There should be only a few issues, if any, if the pre-launch testing was thorough.

Post-Launch Check

- Verify that all forms function correctly. Verify the proper company member receives the information from the form and the site sends the visitor to the "thank you" page after sending the form.
- Site has SSL certificate. There will be a padlock on the left side of the browser's location (address) bar.

- Check internal links throughout the site.
- Check social media links.
- Check all links to external sites and make certain they open in a new browser window.
- Check call-to-action links.
- Check newsletter (or other lead generator) sign-up link.
- Check appearance of the website on all devices.
- Check appearance of the website on the three major browsers: Chrome, Safari and Firefox.
- Verify contact information on the website: phone and address.
- Verify your website speed. Check it with PageSpeed Insights or GTMetrix. Page speed has an impact on how long visitors stay on the site, how many of the visitors convert into paying customers and where you rank organic search.
- Check copyright date. Should include start to current year.
- Meta Title and Page Descriptions: Each page should have its own unique title and description. You are able to view them through your browser. If you are using Safari, for instance, simply go to the Safari tool bar, click "Developer," click "Page Source." They should appear in the code.
- Verify you have access to Google Analytics.
- Verify Google Analytics is collecting information.

Your assignment is almost over.

PRESS ON...

21
_____

THE NEW WEBSITE IS LIVE

What an experience! Congratulations! You succeeded to manage the development of the company's new website.

This book's information is intended to make one's endeavor easy, educational and successful! An attractive, functional, user-friendly and effective website reflects your success.

Having armed yourself with proper knowledge before you started, the journey became easier.

You completed your assignment!

Relax awhile before learning what could be your next assignment.

With your new set of skills, education and experience, you might like to take on the responsibilities of keeping in touch with your website designer/developer to keep the site current with information and technology.

Since there was no one else in the company to take on the responsibility of the business website design, maybe you are the only one to continue with the next steps.

22

THE NEXT STEP

After the website is online, don't ignore it.

This book helped you develop the best website to make your business a success. You created a website that engages your clients and provides many features and opportunities for them to buy your products/services and to contact you. But this is not the end of the attention a website needs.

The life of this website has just begun. To ignore it now will only waste the cost of the website and the hard work you gave to the project.

You wouldn't have thousands of expensive, beautiful, four-color brochures printed and then keep them in the box and not distribute them. You don't want to ignore the website.

Since you are in a small company, you are the one most knowledgeable about the website and can be the one to help promote the new website.

The next chapter includes suggestions about steps to take after you develop the website and had a successful launch.

.   .   .

PRESS ON...

23

POST LAUNCH SUGGESTIONS

This chapter contains a short list of chores that will put your website to work for you.

By establishing and executing this small marketing strategy list, you can create an online visibility and bring more potential customers to your website and business.

Let's get started!

Notify All Clients/Customers

Send an announcement to all your clients/customers and vendors announcing the new website. You can send the announcement by email, postcard or letter. The announcement should contain information on how the sites benefits the clients.

Notify Business Associations and Directories

Notify all the trade and business associations where you have a membership. Provide the website's link so they can add it to your company's directory listing on each organization's website and in their printed directory. The more relevant links to a website, the higher it will rank in the search engines.

Add Website Address to Your Company's Printed Materials

Take the time to inventory all the printed materials produced by the company. Include everything from envelopes to invoices.

Note: Every piece of printed matter should have the website address on it.

As each item needs to be reproduced, revise the piece to include the website address. With business cards, it might be wise to have new ones printed immediately with the website address included.

Suggested items of printed matter:

- Letterhead
- Envelopes (all sizes)
- Business cards
- Invoices
- Checks
- Brochures
- Annual reports
- Note pads
- Price lists
- Company profile
- Order forms
- Catalogs
- Flyers
- Direct mail pieces
- Labels
- Signs
- Maps
- Company cars
- Company vans

- Company trucks

Specialty Advertising

Don't forget to add the website address to specialty advertising items.

Specialty advertising is another way to help prospective customers know your web address. This is where creativity will render no limits. Some possibilities for specialty advertising:

- Pens
- Pencils
- Ballcaps
- Golf shirts
- Golf balls
- Golf tees
- Golf towels
- Place mats
- Auto plates
- Mugs
- Clocks
- Card decks
- Jackets
- Paper weights

Establish Social Media Accounts

Participation in LinkedIn, Twitter, Facebook, Instagram and other social media websites helps provide a path to your business website.

Social media also provides an opportunity to provide backlinks to your website. (Google likes proper backlinks.) The use of social media is one of the most cost effective efforts you can make.

Social media marketing is a great promotional tool to reach thousands of potential customers too.

Start Blogging

A blog is a great way to add new and original content to your website regularly. This shows you are adding fresh content for visitors plus you are adding more pages to your website which Google and other search engines can index.

This area doesn't have to be called a blog. You can name it "News" or "Articles."

Both your visitors and Google like the fact that your website is being updated frequently with new content.

Start Reviewing Your Google Analytics

Your Google Analytics account should have been set up earlier and the code should be on all the pages of the website. It is time to review the analytics.

Google provides several videos to help you use and understand the reports.

You'll learn how to navigate the Google Analytics interface and reports and tp set up dashboards and shortcuts. The course will also show how to analyze basic audience, acquisition, and behavior reports, and set up goals and campaign tracking.

FINAL THOUGHTS

The experiences with my clients inspired me to develop the contents in this book. As a website designer/developer, I have been interviewing the clients for over 20 years in order to determine their objectives, goals and solutions for producing successful websites.

It Was a Novelty to be on the Internet

Commercialization of the Internet began to grow in 1995 and Netscape, a web browser, developed the SSL which made it safer to conduct financial transactions online. Both eBay and Amazon started to grow their online presence in 1995.

In the late 1990s, they considered a business with an Internet presence to be innovative, successful and on the edge of the new technology. It certainly wasn't the competitive Internet of today.

Google went online in 1998 and revolutionized the way Internet users found information online.

It's a Necessity to have an Internet Presence

By 2000 it was no longer just a novelty to be online with a business; it became a necessity to be online.

The Internet will continue to grow and innovations will continue to amaze us. Today, the business website is the hub of its marketing. It is essential for a business to have an online presence but an online presence is not enough. You need a successful online presence.

How do you get a successful online presence?

- Be visible in the search engines.
- Be fast loading for mobile users.
- Quickly show visitors if your product or services are for them.
- Compel visitors to reach out to your business.

IF YOU WOULD PLEASE...

IF THIS BOOK was a help to you, I will be grateful if you took a few minutes to write a review on Amazon.

When you leave a comment on Amazon, the world's largest bookseller, it makes a huge difference to help new readers find my books.

Your review would make my day!

Thank you so much!

ABOUT THE AUTHOR

Frankie Foster is a website designer/developer with over 20 years of experience creating websites for small to medium-sized businesses. She has been responsible for the copywriting and the technical SEO for most of the websites she designed.

She builds each website with the latest SEO technical standards and the SEO changes Google establishes to better refine results based on the user's search intent. She has a proven track record of getting her clients' sites ranked on the first page of Google's results.

Her website expertise includes website design, development and search engine optimization. Additional services she offers are logo design, print and digital design and marketing materials.

Throughout her career she has presented seminars to various business associations and groups about the value of a business's online presence and how to make it work for the company.

She held board positions on the Dublin Chamber of Commerce (Dublin, Ohio), Dublin Arts Council and the National Association of the Remodeling Industry (NARI), Central Ohio Chapter. She received the Dublin Chamber of Commerce "Business Person of The Year" and NARI's "President's Award."

Frankie began her website company in 1997 in Dublin, Ohio after a career as a professional photographer who specialized in portraits, products and industrial photography.

Photography clients ranged from local startup companies to national and international corporations such as The Limited, Turner Construction, Honda, Kinetic Noise Control and Ashland Chemical.

Nationally, she earned the recognition from the Professional Photographers of America as a "Qualified Commercial and Industrial Photographer."

The expertise she brought from the photography career was an insight into the businesses. The insights provide today's clients with a perspective vital to producing a successful website.

As a website designer/developer, she does the same accurate job of portraying business images as she did when she was a photographer —she is simply using different tools.

Websites:

For more information about business websites, visit:

Create a Successful Business Website at

https://businesswebsitetips.com

For website design service, visit:

Website Design by Frankie Foster at

https://thebytesite.com

MY FREE GIFT TO YOU

When you subscribe to my weekly email newsletter packed with information about website sites for small businesses, you will receive for free a copy of *8 Costly and Common Website Mistakes Made by Small Businesses*.

This short, concise book shows business owners, managers and marketers some major website mistakes and how to correct them. You can download the book to your computer.

DOWNLOAD HERE

https://businesswebsitetips.com

Printed in Great Britain
by Amazon

64171998R00057